On Radical Noticing

On Radical Noticing

poems and reflections by

David Breeden

SHANTI ARTS PUBLISHING

BRUNSWICK, MAINE

On Radical Noticing: Poems and Reflections

Published by Shanti Arts Publishing

Designed by Shanti Arts Designs

Cover image: Adobe Contributor / 806307088
/ stock.adobe.com

Unless otherwise noted, translations are by the author.

Shanti Arts LLC
193 Hillside Road
Brunswick, Maine 04011
shantiarts.com

Printed in the United States of America

ISBN: 978-1-962082-32-7 (softcover)

Library of Congress Control Number: 2024941393

for the searchers

Think about how many things happen inside each
of us every split-second. Things that concern the
body and things that concern the consciousness.

When you think in this way, you will be amazed
at all the things that come into existence in this all,
in this totality that we call the cosmos, all existing
at the same moment.

—Marcus Aurelius, *Meditations*, 6.25

Many Things—are fruitless—
'Tis a Baffling Earth—

—Emily Dickinson, #614

Contents

❧

THREE **POEMS ABOUT WRITING POEMS**

❧

FOUR **INSEPARABLE (AND INSEPARABLY) TOGETHER**

FIVE **THE ULTIMATE ULTIMACY**

ACKNOWLEDGEMENTS

The RavensPerch (theravensperch.com):
  "The Ashes As It Were";
  "Gulp";
  "Hey, America, Your Rebar is Showing";
  "An Old Chair Calls";
  "On Singing to the Crickets"; and
  "A Voice of Experience"

Author's Note

This is a book about radical noticing. What's that? Radical noticing is a term used in mindfulness and contemplative practices. It refers to a state of heightened awareness and deep observation of one's present-moment experience, encompassing both internal and external phenomena.

In radical noticing, we cultivate a deliberate nonjudgmental attentiveness to sensory perceptions, thoughts, emotions, and bodily sensations. Radical noticing involves fully immersing oneself in the present moment, with a curious, open mind.

The term "radical" implies going to the root or essence of something. In the context of noticing, it suggests a profound level of attentiveness that goes beyond clichés, stereotypes, and surface-level observations. Radical noticing involves perceiving the subtle details, nuances, and interconnections that might typically go unnoticed in the midst of a stressful day.

Through the practice of radical noticing, we become more aware of our habitual patterns, our biases, assumptions, and automatic reactions. By observing thoughts, sensations, and emotions without judgment or attachment, we can develop a heightened appreciation of the richness and interconnectedness of experience.

The goal of radical noticing is continuous wonder, imagination, and gratitude. What many label the mystical state.

Radical noticing is about paying attention. Paying attention as a spiritual practice, a practice of attention, of directed consciousness.

Along the way, I will discuss how I have managed to more-or-less live an aesthetic life and a life in aesthetics through poetry and philosophy. Imagination.

The following consists of snapshots, sketches, AI experiments, and word doodles in time having to do with as much of everything as I can understand, and some things I can't.

ONE

BEAUTY IS TRUTH

✤

It is difficult
to get the news from poems
                yet people[1] die miserably every day
                            for lack
of what is found there.[2]

—William Carlos Williams

---

1. "men"
2. https://poets.org/poem/asphodel-greeny-flower-excerpt

IMPERMANENCE

Grecian Urn.[3] That
>sounds so much richer than
>>Greek Urn, huh?

Timeless? No,
>Beauty isn't. But it lingers,
>>enduring enough ages,
encased, confined in glass walls

that is seems true,
>yeah, because
>it's old. Seriously,
>>does beauty reveal truth
beneath its surface?

Only shallow truths, perhaps,
>not where the
>>meanings are, as Emily D.
once said.

The nature of existence,
>of the human condition,
the essence of reality . . .

what can catch that
but a verb. *Being*, maybe.
Being.

---

3. "Beauty is truth, truth beauty,—that is all
>Ye know on earth, and all ye need to know."

>>—from "Ode on a Grecian Urn" by John Keats

Was Keats hopeful
        that poetry upholds it all,
                undergirds it all?

Sure, there's a philosophy of poetry,
        a poetics of resemblance
                driven by the power
of imagination and its senses.

Seriously, did Keats think that
        contemplating beauty awakens
                some higher consciousness,

something beyond subjectivity,
        beyond his own sensibilities?
                Cultivated, refined.

"Beauty is truth, truth beauty."
        It's true, in the realm of Art, anyway.
                But in the underground market of antiquities,

values run to another sort, and

truth may be truth,
        and beauty may be beauty,
but the two shall never meet.

IMPERMANENCE CAN-CAN

Impermanence has an attitude.
     Can't debate about that. Always
          it says, Going! Going! Gone!

It says, Missed it, didn't you?
     Impermanence has an attitude.
          Sure, you wanna smack its smirky

face. But what's the point? Then
     it only wins bigger. Going . . .
          Impermanence has an attitude,

and smacking only makes it
     haughtier somehow. Yes, it
          just loves you angry. Boiling.

Are you pissed yet that you are
     aging? Weakening? Dying?
          Has It sunk in yet? Are you

pissed at the presumption?
     Good. You've got it: Going . . .
          But you ain't gone.

Hug it:

     dance as only impermanence can!

Unpatterned Dreams

In dreams, when
      beauty pops in,
specters, shadows, stories sashaying
      around, then time

      loses the thread[4]
      and the loom

embraces
      its memories.
         Flickers and flashes

still light the way to guide the tread.

---

4. Imagining that there is a beauty that time cannot steal,
    specters cast their wide, elusive shadows
        onto a human tapestry woven without design.
         yet, flickers, flashes from the flames
    onto life's tapestry and the purposes we pull into thread.

An Old Chair Calls

Notice and live,
        the poets call.

See and change,
        cries the intricate

        weave of an old
chair's seat. The

        often un-named
thing at the center

of why. Twine in
        an intricate weave,

twinned into
        a usefulness

that calls out: see.
        Notice and change.

TRUTH CLAIMS

the beauty of poetry
    is that it makes no claims

    about truth
    but only beauty

which is truth as
poets know

    or at least that's
        what so many

poets have said
    they know

to be true

GEMLIKE

In the conclusion to his book of essays *The Renaissance: Studies in Art and Poetry*, Walter Pater (1839–1894) wrote:

> This at least of flamelike our life has, that it is but the
> concurrence, renewed from moment to moment, of
> forces parting sooner or later on
> their ways.

Yes, it's all a swirl. Our interior lives—what Pater calls the "inward world of thought and feeling"—is a "whirlpool" that "is still more rapid, the flame more eager and devouring." The way to live is with both focus and abandon. Pater wrote:

> Some spend this life in listlessness,
> some in high passions,
> the wisest, at least among the children of this world,
> in art and song. For our one chance lies in expanding
> that interval, in getting as many pulsations as possible
> into the given time. Great
> passions may give us this
> quickened sense of life,
> ecstasy and sorrow of love,
> the various forms of enthusiastic activity, disinterested
> or otherwise, which come naturally to many of us.
> Only be sure it is passion—
> that it does yield you
> this fruit of a quickened,
> multiplied consciousness.

Of such wisdom, the poetic passion, the desire of
beauty,
the love of art for its own sake, has most. For art comes
to you proposing frankly to give nothing but the
highest
quality to your moments as they pass, and simply
for
those moments' sake.

My favorite passage, and my guide to what writing means to me:

To burn always with this hard, gemlike flame,
to maintain this ecstasy, is success in life.
In a sense it might even be said that our failure
is to form habits: for, after all, habit is relative
to a stereotyped world, and meantime it is only
the roughness of the eye that makes any two
persons, things, situations, seem alike.[5]

---

5.   https://www.gutenberg.org/files/2398/2398-h/2398-h.htm

Too Solid

"Now more than ever
      seems it rich to die,"
            wrote Keats, young man

with no future. "To cease
      upon the midnight
            with no pain," wrote

Keats from his too,
      too solid flesh
            betraying him.

TWO

CONSTRUCTING/DECONSTRUCTING THE SELF

Two things fill the mind with ever new and increasing wonder and awe, the more often and steadily we reflect upon them: the starry heavens above me and the moral law within me.

—Immanuel Kant, *Critique of Practical Reason*, 1788

Only I'm imaginary,
make-believe beyond belief,
so fictitious that it hurts.

—Wistawa Szymborska, "Over Wine"

PLACE

I awoke
       to consciousness
       watching
            yellow dust
swirl in our wake,

our wake on a gravel road,
       the popping
            of random rocks
against the car's floorboard.

I hear
       the slow chug
       of a two-cylinder
            engine,
            John Deere,
& a low note,
       a single
       violin. It's
            playing . . .
            what?
some scherzo or other,

a tune
       better played
       on a banjo.

       I see the shimmer
            of a black snake
                 moving fast
       across the road

Yellow dust rattles
        onto the weed stalks.
                I blink into consciousness.

I am a child of the soil.[6]

---

6.   Doesn't every event take place somewhere? Seems to me the
statement makes sense. I'm supposing even those events that take place
everywhere, such as the expansion of the universe, also do actually take
place somewhere . . .

LESSON LEARNED

"Mistrust is the intelligence,"
wrote Peter Sloterdijk,[7] "of

       the disadvantaged." Just
       like that—it's what you learn

from being poor: don't
trust rich. Don't trust

       power. Don't trust
       learning. The wisdom
         is in the

don't trust. It's a lesson
learned soon enough,

       and a lesson not forgot.

---

7.   Peter Sloterdijk (1947–) is a German philosopher and cultural critic.

ALL THOSE

All those moments of consciousness.
All those
      moments
    of consciousness
all along a whole life long.

How can we ever hold so many thoughts?
How can
      we ever
      hold so
            many thoughts

so long?
A life
      out of moments.
      A life
out of lines jotted,

lines jotted
      in hope they
      might be
            poetry.

I Used To Be a . . .

In the 1970s I worked at a small radio station in a small town not far from our family farm. I enjoyed working as a disc jockey. It's how I paid my tuition to the local community college.

One thing I did as a DJ was entertain at the local nursing home once a month, playing some old music and making a few jokes. One thing I carried away from that experience has stuck with me over the years, and that was that so many of the old folks would start conversation with "I used to be a . . . ." Clearly, these folks had identified their self-hood—their essences—with what they did for a living. This was especially true of old men.

I determined that I would never be that guy.

What we "are"—what we are in essence and authenticity—is what we are in this moment (meaning every moment of our existence). Moment-to-moment is how we live. Inhale, exhale, repeat. One heartbeat, the next. Until they cease.

For a long time people have used the metaphor of theatre to talk about how human beings take action in the world: "a poor player (actor) that struts and frets (their) hour upon the stage and is then no more."

GULP

Now, each
       moment
each line
       I think
—the rest
       is gravy
       the rest
       is gravy

Just like
       it's always
been
       just as

it's always been

the sooner
       we realize
       the sooner
we live

LET'S GET THIS STRAIGHT (PHENOMENOLOGY 101)

Here I am with my opposable thumbs.
    Through no fault of my own. I'm here.

Here we all are with our opposable thumbs.
    Through no fault of our own. We're here.

Through no thought of my own
    I'm thinking all these things. I'm here.

Through no thought of our own
    we're thinking all these things. We're here.

It merely is what it is. That.
    Yes, it's that. It's only that I'm here.

It's merely that you're here.
    Here I am. I'm with what I am.

Here we are. We're with what we are.
    Through no thought of our own.

Here I am.
    Here we are.

Through no action of my own.
    Through no action of our own.

Here I am.
      Here we are.

Here I am with . . .
      Here we are with . . .

Here all of us are.
      With.

Here we are. With each other. Welcome.
We're all here. Through no fault of our own.
      Cut the blame. Be. Here.

On This Dawn to Be

"Bliss it was in that dawn to be alive," Henry Wordsworth wrote in *The Prelude* as he reflected on his youth—"But to be young was very heaven."

When I first read those lines, when I was in my twenties, I envied Wordsworth. To have lived in an age where possibility seemed possible. To have been young with a dream of revolution and a just society.

Society felt hardly changeable to me when I read those lines. T. S. Eliot's "The Waste Land" felt more apropos. Or Ginsberg's "Howl." But most of all Jim Morrison's lyrics from "The End:"

> Lost in a Roman wilderness of pain
> And all the children are insane
> All the children are insane
> Waiting for the summer rain . . .

Yes, that's more what it felt like on my dawn to be alive, and I remember the first time the dam broke and I began writing in the ecstasy of inspiration. I was smoking a joint and I began to scrawl in pencil on lined paper with that song in my head. I wrote pages and pages of bad verse into the early morning hours.

I lost those pages long ago. But the ecstasy of writing away anxiety and pain . . . I never lost that feeling.

Yes, to be young can be very hell. But in the forty years and more since I wrote my first lines, poetry has saved me more than once from the ravages of clinical depression and of life.

Today, I sip my coffee and write in the mornings,
not in darkness. My fingers fly across the keyboard,
unencumbered by cigarettes or the sullen resistance
of a manual typewriter.

Yes, still I write; I still write to survive. I write a poem
called "That Perfect Sunlight:"

> Fat old men
> write poetry too;
> perhaps we shouldn't,
> but we do.
>
> Age and aches
> fade in a poem;
> almost like we've put
> some wisdom on.
>
> Time and mistakes
> sink in the lines
> that reel out as if
> we're creating time.
>
> And more time
> for us to write
> that perfect
> sunlight.

Oh, on this sunset to be alive. And to be old . . . someway
toward very heaven.

MARX AND MUSSOLINI FOLD THE FLAG IN BLINDING WHITE GLOVES

On a night full
    of dreaming
    there's the blind-
        ing white gloves

    to say it's
time to full-
    stop, stop

the fortune-
    telling at last,
the hope-

    full fore-
        telling that
leads to

the usual kill-
        ing sprees.

Karl did it—
    like any other
        prophet—wish-

ful thinking
that leads to
    hopeful kill-

        ing sprees.

Benito did it—
        in reverse—
but the same

wishful think-
            ing that leads
to the usual

            killing sprees

that on nights
        full of dream-
ing lead to find-
        ing blind-

ing white
gloves.

A VOICE OF EXPERIENCE

There is no monastery like
    A bus moving through
The American night

TOWER

A picnic around the tower,
        grass as lush as duck down,
                but dark clouds rising

                like a locust storm.
                        How *noir*
        some folks in hats remark.

        The tower wrecks dreams,

yet, the seeds of some
        solace and resolve floats,
                resistant to antihistamines.

Run Yer Run. Be

What was that big circle
you thought you'd run?
One big oval or
some figure eight?

Sure, come to that,
it's all about the
time. Which. You know.
Uh, doesn't exist.

It's all about the time,
which doesn't exist,
and all about the

future. Which does
not either.

What?
What's the big deal
about the moment?

The big

circle we'd all
like to run. One
big oval or
some figure eight.

SOMEWHERE YOURSELF

No, you will not appear
on *The Ed Sullivan Show*.

That was about others,
not about your self.

All that is over now.
No, you will not appear

on the Ed Sullivan Show
but you have not disappeared.

Your future is
somewhere else.

You will now appear
somewhere else

in another time
that is your own.

THE ASHES AS IT WERE

Still I get my dad's
USW@Work
magazine long after
he's dead. I don't
tell them. I like
getting it. Seeing
what people like
my dad look like
nowadays. Working

class. Working
      steel. When you
           handle burning
                 steel every day,
           you're gonna
      get burned. It's
a question of

time and how
many times. And
how much. I run

my finger down
      the list on the back,
           the ones killed
      at work this
year. It was never
      you, dad, though
           my kid
      visions flashed
with your fiery

death. Never you,
                but for so many.
       How many? I
count them each
                issue. I count them
         each year on the back
of your magazine, dad,
because you knew that,
          like so much of sacrifice,
                it all runs together
          after a while. Into
the ashes as it were.

AXIOLOGY: WHAT IS OF VALUE IN THE WORLD?

My story I carry with me,[8]
    my stories and my
        elaborations,
        evasions,
        erasures.
    Semantic presuppositions.
    Cultural presuppositions.

Hey, erasures, come on
along. This is one
story you don't wanna
miss. You can fill in
some smokey mood,
some dark 'n' stormy
ambiance. Even a hall
of mirrors to be erased by.

"For ever, I shall be a stranger to myself"
Albert Camus wrote in "The Myth of Sisyphus"

"Finally, I choose freedom.
For even if justice is not realized,
freedom maintains the power
of protest against injustice and
keeps communication open" wrote
Albert Camus in *The Rebel*.

---

8. Story, Story, Poem
    Many, perhaps most, people experience their lives as narrative. Like in
    a novel or film. Sometimes they change the narrative, but it is still based
    in the idea—framed by the idea—of a story. Upon reflection, I suppose
    that I have lived in my body as a lyric poem. I didn't hear an epic. A lyric
    poem. That smallest and most delicate of songs, images in song.

In the ol' America
the story was all
about expansion

In the now America
the story is all
about connection

        Out and in.

But, unlike breath,
        now ol' America
            will only connect.

INNER WORK

Shout into the
cavern of your

    weakness.

    Hear the echo,
        how it comes back
            strong. Listen—

    What do the rocks
know that

we've forgotten?

An Opening

You are the riveted steel.
You are the stainless,
embossed to shining.

     You are the network.
     You are the intricacies
     in the mechanized.

          You are, yet you
          might be more—
          Search the interstices.

Find,

          find the silence
          before the wires
          shut again.

KNOWING

You know
        the night. It waits
                outside.
You can love it,
or you can run.

The night don't care
      who you are—Each
             day you're
gonna
take on

the empire.

Broken Chapels, Same Difference

Oh, little ol' church, what can I say to you
with your walls rotted and your bell gone?

> I can offer a whispered poem,
> little ol' church, to your
> splintered pews, in rows
> like the dead outside. Here

people felt for their souls,
for solace, a presence

maybe. Through it all—
—meaning joy, sorrows,
hope, despair—little ol' church

> the burden,
> the whispers
> the sunlit

fragments, as close to stained

glass as may be, colors on
the floorboards, a
solipsism
oh, little ol' church,

you've seen it all—walls broken, bell gone.

Take a Number, Be a Number, Do a Number

Sure, we all must settle
        into our graves. Some
        take it fast, some slow,
but all will join in the

dance soon enough.

Join in the dance,
            all have done, all
            the people all the way
back. Join in the dance

that sends trembles,
        echos, the thud of feet
                into whatever abyss
may be somewhere.

Join in the dance.
Disturb the abyss.
        If anything seems amiss
                    it's only the lies

you've memorized.

ŚŪNYATĀ (EMPTINESS)

> The limits of nirvana are the limits of samsara. No difference.
> —Nagarjuna (ca. 15–250 CE)

Go ahead, try to awake to
what is not there, not
there in anything that
might be called a thing.
To say it's empty is only

> to say it's real, solid like
> the concrete you wrote
> your name in on that
> afternoon long ago.

> To say it is real is only
> to say that it's empty.
> Try to awake to feel the
> empty—like a rusted tin
> bucket shot full of holes—

leaking any self that might
imagine a self; leaking *I*,
leaking *me*; leaking *mine*;
leaking any thing. Oh, and self.

A Greeting: Summing It Up

I am an old farmer
and I come to you
       for no other reason,
       no other excuse, but
       that here I am and I
have something to say,

as do we all.
       As do we all.

I come to you
as the old movies
       go—in peace; a
       foreigner; an alien
       in whatever place
any of us find

ourselves. We all
       do. As do we all.

Yes, there are others
       walking upstairs,
       down. And sometimes
       nobody even close.
That's how it is in
       being. There and

here. That's how it
        is in what we perhaps
        will call life after all.
        We're here, for no
other reason than
        that we are here.

We have no other
        excuse but that here
        we are. And we have
        something to say:

Stranger in a strange land
        Stranger is a strange land
            estrange
                extraneous

BOTCHED NAIL

A fixed human nature
      fixed a lot
            of problems—religion,
philosophy. When
that nail comes
      unstuck—subjective
self claims the rights
      and the wrongs.
            The nail that slipped.

THREE

POEMS ABOUT WRITING POEMS

Adventure most unto itself
The Soul condemned to be—
Attended by a single Hound
Its own identity.

—Emily Dickinson, #822

So It Is

So it is I write—no ideas
        but in things; not irritably
             reaching
                        for certainty. I write words

    without much trusting them

without much more to
        go on than to ask what other
             conveyance might there be?

        Beaten by capitalism, necessarily.
            Searching for the beatific vision, always.
                Grasping for the words
                to catch the image
                of every little thing.

            Convinced that this is the only way for me.

TO WRITE POETRY IS

To write poetry is
to give up

even an inkling of
          what happens

next. To surrender

wondering even that
anyone will try,

anyone will care
enough to trace

          the dark runnels
          where we cry.

Symbols Don't Mean Beans

> "The creation of yet another culture, a new story to
> explain the world and our participation in it, a new
> value system with images and symbols that connect
> us to each other and to the planet."
> —Gloria Anzaldúa

I.

Symbols & metaphors
don't go away nicely.

    You can sell your birth-
    right for porridge; you
        can sell your cow
        for beans—Somehow,

somehow symbols will eat
    your lunch, and the
        heavy boat of metaphor

will sink in as concrete
    boats do. They
        will leave you
gasping for air.

II.

Symbols & metaphors
        don't go away nicely:
        We try to chuck
them with words,

words, words,
but symbols—
like old tires,
like fan belts—

don't rot. Much.

III.

Symbols & metaphors & similes,
even, don't go away nicely.

        What do you read?
        Words, words.

        What's the matter?
The matter? It matters!

Symbols & metaphors & similes.

IV.

Symbols & metaphors
& similes & clichés
don't go away nicely—

       they say who
       is in, who out;

       who gets hurt,
       who gets beans.

What do the symbols
       mean, I mean, when
           used out loud and

for something? Who
       gets ahead? Which
           clichés click? Who

gets hurt? What does it
       matter? Yes, and metaphors
           mix and some become dead letters.

V.

Symbols & metaphors
       & similes & clichés
       are dead
       and buried but
come back

       ready to kick
       ass again.

Perceptions—
          what do
          they say
          "yes" to,
          "no" to?

Meanings.
          What will
                    they start
          and put a
                    stop to?

VI.

Symbols & metaphors
& similes & cliches
don't go away nicely.

          Don't go away
          at all. And one's

          freedom is
                    another's cell,
                              n'est-ce pas?
What are the
thoughts set

          stirring? What are
                    the symbols, et cetera
                              marching about?

Who tells the story?
Who is listening?

Who's left out?
               Who's hurt? What
                              power and which
prisons? Which
empty alleys?

VII.

If you ain't
got beans
you don't
throw 'em
in a pot.

VIII.

Symbols & images
& all those other things
don't go away nicely.

               & even when you
               see their backs . . .

They will
               come back.

HERE'S YOUR CHANCE

A work of art is a chance
       to rework the wounds
of time, of self. A work

       of art is a shot at getting
            to a true image, a right
                 symbol, a just world, even.

At the frayed edges, artists
       swirl; loving, intricate spirits
searching. Every work is

       a shot at getting it right.
            Meaning the world, just,
                true. At least in the eclectic

swirl of the artist's mind.

Signs, Signs[9]

Yes, I know. I've realized
that these words I do,
these words I push so hard
against the page, are

      squiggles only. Only
      squiggles. No thoughts.
      No sweat. Only abstracted
      marks pushed into paper.

I know. I've realized that
no emotion stays here.
No blood flows from

the words I write—wound.
Blood. Too, too much.
I know. I've realized that
squiggles won't add up

to the life lost making

green logs into the fire,

into spaces, blanks,
silences, kerfuffles.
Drawing the sounds

we imagine words
make and meanings
we imagine this, that

---

9. Naming

sound has. Unlearning
what has been
heaped, thrown like

shovelfuls of coal into
that infernal engine.

them. I know. I've realized
too late and not soon
enough where the lies lie.

Still, I make them. As if
they alone are life.

Among the Lines

Art so often
       condemning
              what is, so often

panegyric to
       what might be.

Here among
       the lines I am
              safe—long lines,

       short. It's me
              who decides

for a change
       from life. Calling
              out what is.

Mapping what
       might be.

I so often
       am not. Art
              so often is.

HERE'S HOW IT IS, WCW

(A Lyric of These States)

Here's how
        it is—W.C.W.

poet of my
        dreams,
                you

showed me
        this
                path but

no way
        out,
                only some

perhaps alright
                ways to

write, oh, I dunno
        the lyric of,

ya know: These States

        sort of thing

Art Is

What is it about Art
that both calls us in
and calls us out?

       That creates both
       hope and an elusive
       dream of wholeness?

Art creates at once
hunger and satiety. Both
desert and dessert,

despair and dreams at
what we human beings
can do and be.

       Making art, sharing art
       for artist and audience—
       for humanity—is ancient

and basic and sublime.
Art guides us to a place
where expression,

artistic, personal, happens,
beautifully, spontaneously.
Art takes us to the place

       of our true selves,
       in being, in doing,
       and in the world.

FREE OF BOXES

Can you write in the box,
       any box? Any little room
               that might get thrown

your way in the brutality
       of absolute form? In the
               simplicity of getting caught.

Can you write your way out
       of any room, of any box that
               might get thrown at you?

Sure. Yes. Write and speak
       the words saying, Yes,
               I am free of boxes. Go!

SIGN DOTTED LINE

That's the poet's contract, huh?
To say what can't be said and

      to say what can't be, which is,
      yes, prophecy. Ain't that the
      deal the poet signs up for—

Write these things
because these things

are these things and
happen in this life.

      Poet, priest, prophet, sayer
      of those things that are not said,

cannot be said, and the sayer
of the sad and the ecstatic.

ON SINGING TO THE CRICKETS

When there are so many,
      in dark drawers,
      in jumbled files,
so many unread,
      unheard, why write
      another poem?

          The poet sang, and . . .
              crickets.

Why sing another song
      when the echo will be
      almost inevitably
          crickets?

They won't clap.
They murmur all the while.

      A tough crowd,
         crickets.

Yet they are there,
      singing their own songs,
         absorbed

in their own their own horizons
with their own winter coming.

          The poet sang, and . . .
            so did the crickets.

Where're You At, Apollinaire?

Apollinaire, In his poem "Zone,"
     liberation, adventure, transcendence,
aviation, progress, boundaries
     crossed, almost
          transgressed might we
    almost say?
At the least, momentarily transcended.

        Aviation! even better
        than an automobile!

Freedom, possibilities, thought the poet,
imagined the poet who
would get shot in the head
in the trenches.
Shrapnel in the head in the trenches.

     Imagine that.

     Taking flight.

Where're you at, Apollinaire?
     In the "Zone" I guess. Easy guess.
       You dared to declare
       liberation in a space,
   a place you'd never be.
Didn't it feel so possible . . . aviation,

          sky's the limit 'n' all that.
      Possibilities in the almost possible,
         where the dreams are.

And in trenches, well.
Imagine that. Taking flight
into shrapnel and chaos,
        juxtaposing, on the fly,
        freedom and
the horrors of flight.
        Apollinaire, wordsmith,
                rhythm unbound,
                        aviator's spirit in the infartry mud.
                                In the "Zone"
                                even after
                                he got shot
                                in the head.
                                Shrapnel in
                                the brain.

        He found his way,
        like every they,
        embracing the finesse,
                                Where're you at, Apolliraire?
                Your words echo in an air
                where art and whatever happens.
Go ahead,

                                harmonize, take fight.

FOUR

INSEPARABLE (AND INSEPARABLY) TOGETHER

The glacier knocks in the cupboard,
The desert sighs in the bed,
And the crack in the tea-cup opens
A lane to the land of the dead.

—W.H. Auden, "As I Walked Out One Evening"

HEY, AMERICA, YOUR REBAR IS SHOWING

Hey, America, yer rebar is showin'.
Used to be that looked like tomorrow,
looked like progress comin'. But
all the rust is tellin'
another kinda tale.

Hey, America, your rebar is showin'.
We the people
know it's a lie now,
all that you've said
about equality and such.

Hey, America, your rebar is showin'.
It's not a good look on you.
Means you gave up tryin'
to make anything but money.

Hey, America, yer rebar's showin'.
It ain't a good look,
all that rust over the steel
where plaster coulda been.

DESIDERATA

There is who the person is.
There is who the artist is.

There is what the person says.
There is what the artist says.

The ideal: these are the same.
The real: these are often different.

This is a challenge for the person.
This is a tragedy for the artist.

This is a challenge for the art.
This can be a tragedy for the art.

To find the artist, find the art.
Find the art. The person . . .

We wish the person
the best, but we know

the person, if the person
is or was an artist,

lived for the art. That
is where to start. There

is the best of ourselves.

Days Like

Some days, don't
nobody come along.

       Some days,
       somebody comes along.

         Cain't never tell
one day to the nex'.

One day, three cars come along.

Boy-yee that was a busy one.

Mos' days, though, don't
nobody come along.

       Some days,
       mos' anybody'll come along.

Cain't tell
         one day ta-'nother.

Cain't tell.

THE UNIQUENESS PARADOX

Oh, my, my,
oh, my my,
we're all individuals—
that ain't no lie.

Oh, me, me,
oh, me, me,
how are a bunch of individuals
gonna be free?

Oh, we, we,
oh, we, we,
we all gotta figure
how to agree.

Oh, us, us,
oh, us, us,
how good it is
when we build trust.

WRITING ON

Perhaps I wish this were a hill
       and a chance to survey the scene.

       Perhaps I wish this were a mountain
       and a chance to survey everywhere.

              Perhaps wherever I am
              I can't see down,
              and I can't see back.

Perhaps I can't see much
at all. Perhaps.
Yet I write on, hoping

to see—perhaps not back,
       perhaps not forward. Perhaps

              somewhere. Maybe here.

Riffs Off a Line by Camus

in stones and flesh
        our journey lies
bound under stars

                                    where destiny cries
               truths birth-certified

                                for stones
             ancient guardians, shown
resilience

close at hand
        frail vessels
                       embracing a world that
                                    wrestles

an undeniable realm
                          warmth
                               stars above
those touchable
                    truths, heart's raw
embrace

             flesh
                      gaze
uncover in

                    this Kosmic
                        dance we discover

LIFE AND OPTIONS

Option One:

Get born.
Want.
Want.
Do.
Want.
Want.
Die.

Option Two:

Get born.
Want.
Want.
Contemplate.
Do.
Do.
Do.
Die.

ETHOS (ἦθος)[10]

After even words
      fade and only
           the body's truth
is solid enough,

boundaries merge,
      existence reaches
           to embrace essence.
Those ethereal

moments, being, essence,
      an intricacy
beyond words,
a Kosmic song

embracing all,
      infinite, no limits.

Is that you
      there sittin'
           like a sittin' hen
                on what you are?

---

10.   customs, habits, moral values that define a person, group, or culture; a term usefully used instead of the ubiquitous "spirit"

It Appears to Be Happening That

Some things are happening
       and some things are not. It's

hard to know the difference
       between the same-'ol same-'ol

and the new-fangled flush.

AXIOLOGY[11]

Axiology, axiology,
      it's got nothin' to do
      with axes or apology
but rather how we
      hew our values
            and decide what to
chop away.

Axiology. Ask me
      how I prioritize,
      enterprise, and realize
ethical behavior!
      Axiology. It's me
          figuring out how
to live socially

and still be me.
Axiology. It's got

      nothin' to do
          with axes, except
             that it do.

---

11.   Axiology is a branch of philosophy that considers how our values
shape our behavior, decision-making, and judgments of what is good,
beautiful, or morally right, and their opposites. Axiology tends to consider
ethical values, aesthetic values such as beauty and art, and epistemic
(episteme, ἐπιστήμη) values such as truth and knowledge.

Dogged by Automatism We

All around us swirls the news
the news that self interest left
to flow will make things great.
      The news that's not news.
           The news that's not new.

The news that's
the same ol'
same ol' lie.

Henri Bergson said
      dead retain
           for a time
features of the living.[12]

Hard to say he's wrong there.
      Hard to say he's wrong. We
           forget that time
                  freezes motion;
we forget that
           time is never there.
We forge that "a *thing*

is always
a *progress*."

---

12.   Robert French Leavens and Mary Agnes Leavens, editors, *Great Companions: Readings on the Meaning and Conduct of Life from Ancient and Modern Sources, Volume II*. Boston: Beacon Press, 1941. pp. 45-46.

EXPECTATIONS

I just snuffed
a mosquito
on the porch.

      Little guy had
             been buzzing
me a while.

Sorry, friend,
      locked in
             a moment

that didn't go
as planned.

Setting About

> The wise set about creating order out of chaos.
> —*The I Ching*

The wise set about
ordering the farm.
      Where are the snakes,
            where the skunks;
                  where's the alfalfa
      and the stink weed?
The wise, the wise
set about making
      some order out of
            chaos. If I were a turtle
               climbing a mountain
      I guess I'd start at
the bottom first.
If I were a rabbit
      on a mountain
      I suppose I'd start
      my lunch at the base.

OH, AND ANOTHER THING

(After Hafiz)

I.

Has the sun at last
      parted its curtain
            before you & you

have seen in full
      sunlight backstage,
            last breaths, in full

sun dark partings?
      Have you at last
            opened the curtain

at the sunrise of
      your own debut?
            We are all, haven't

you seen, we stage
      hands, ready to
rip the fabric,

      prepared to smile
            in full sun?

II.

I'm not a captain
       for the days of
       wine and roses.
I'm a captain for
       the days of backs
           to the wall—

III.

Oh, & one other thing—
       this particular "I" believes
           that "I" is another
       curtain—construction,
not a thing.
       Real things sting.
       "I"—well—try it.

FIVE

THE ULTIMATE ULTIMACY

One believes in existence;
Another says, "There is nothing!"
Rare is the one who believes in neither.
That one is free from confusion.

—Ashtavakra Gita 18:42, 500 BCE

To be a Flower, is profound
Responsibility

—Emily Dickinson, #1058

We remain unaware of the full extent to which
characteristic concepts and patterns of philosophy
and literature are displaced and reconstituted
theology, or else a secularized form of devotional
experience.

—M. H. Abrams, *Natural Supernaturalism*

Mindfulness and Sense-making

We are interpreting and making sense of the world each and every moment. Generally, this follows predicated patterns: getting up, getting dressed, going out, cooking, consuming. That sort of thing. In these activities, we generally go on auto-pilot. Yet, we are still interpreting and making sense of the world, even when we are going on our clichéd, stereotypic way.

We can, however, interrupt this flow of cliché. This interruption can be the use of a mind-altering substance; it can be mindfulness or a spiritual practice, such as breathing. These practices call attention to the act of interpreting and making sense of the world. Our attention is called to.

We can call these practices of attention. Intentional attention direction. We have stopped in clichés and started considering our reality for sense: why is that shingle askew? What sort of bug is that and why is it doing what it's doing? Why are the clouds doing that? What's that noise? Why am I here?

A neighbor comes out on the stoop and shakes a dust mop into the air. Why? It's a rote activity, most likely. Perhaps the simple joy of pushing a mop has escaped my neighbor.

Many of us live in distraction, chores, enforced activities, drudgery, ads, alerts, messages, interesting stories, alarming stories.

Stop. How are you making sense of your world right now?

Ask yourself: Is the sense I'm making right now actually making sense?

Avoid All

that knock
at your door like the
Fuller Brush[13] man did
when I was a kid.
My mom brushed him

off and bought what
she needed. No up-
sale, Mr. Fuller Brush
Man. Go on down
the road.
Avoid all
religions that knock
at your door when

no one asked.

---

13. Shiny briefcase, Mr. Fuller Brush
Man. Salesman's tie, Mr. Fuller
Brush Man—brooms, dusters,

even brushes, cleaning magic.
He could make dirt scatter. Mr.
Fuller Brush Man. Mr. Fuller

Brush
Man, take your religion
on down the road.

Sitting

stale breath
  stomachs
gurgling

om namah shivaya

the old notes
of breath
of mind

om namah shivaya

words warping
off the rusty nails
  meaning

meaning, bowing
into letters

into sounds
into the stale
  meaning breaths
of asking
& getting just what
the warped words
  asked

om namah shivaya

Nine Propositions Concerning Truth

I.

Perhaps it's true that
    your metaphor is better
        than mine. Yours is truer,

if truer is better. Yet
    might there be another
        truer still? So, is it a pity

    that we are born where
        and when we are born?
            What even is all the

answers?

II.

Here's one motif
that runs and runs:

    When a pauper
    takes to sail,

        and lives to
        come back,

he will be rich
and find his love.

    Clearly. Observe.

III.

at these tree-lined
        streets, flags
                on every house.
Everybody's a

        patriot here,
                marching to
        the drum,
        to the drum
where

IV.

acres of cars,
        trucks, hoods
                up, wait
to lose this
and that
        part forever
                in service of
another
        going on. Observe,

V.

heads that may
embrace
latitudes

must

turn enough
degrees, though

VI.

the bodies
       never last
               so long
as the excuse
       for the killing,

            and

VII.

hanging from a golden
       chain is hanging still.

VIII.

A girl turns the crank
of a jack-in-the-box.

       It makes her smile;
       it makes her wince

in anticipation.

       She turns the crank
       and it will, it
       will jump . . .

IX.

The captain of
        the Golden Dawn
                in the old folk tune

says as his ship goes down—

"I've fished deeper
        waters." Perhaps
                the captain was

exaggerating. After
        all, when do dawns
                go down? Perhaps

he was confused.
        Admit it—as last words,
                they're not so bad.

TRUTH FOR NOW

Speak of truth. Speak of now.
        These are not the same.

These are not the same needs.
        Not the same question. Speak.

Speak now. Truths . . . those perhaps
        will someday be our speaking.

For now—it is only now.

METAPHYSICS, A SUMMARY

Yes, it's nothing.
        No, it's everything.

Yes. No. Right here.
        Right now. No. Or

not. Yes. Now. No.
        Not yet. Or. Or.

Introduction: Time and It Stopping

I.

I have an app that
     names the flowers
          and the weeds.

Even some trees.

And another one
     for the birds. I
          act like Adam in

his big mythic garden,
     nailing the names
          of everything down—

my new apps.

II.

"Nature is a temple,"
     Baudelaire wrote,
          "in which living pillars
sometime give voice
     to confused words . . ."

He called his poem
     "Correspondances."
          But in truth, there

aren't any. The forest[14]
       of symbols is only in
             our minds. And apps.

III.

Isaiah the old prophet yelled,

"All flesh is grass, and
 all the goodliness thereof
 is as the flower of the field:

      The grass withereth,
           the flower fadeth:
                because the spirit of
      the Lord bloweth upon it:
           surely
                the people is grass.
      The grass withereth,
           the flower fadeth . . ."

---

14. A forest at evening,
    soft yellow light falling
    warm on a few leaves,
    the rest already in shadow.

IV.

Yes, all withered;
all faded; the wind,

> the wind blows and
> no rain comes;

withered; faded.
> It's called "time."

V.

Yes, the smell of new-mown grass,
the smell of leather boxed up
and newly opened—they
blend in that day that baffles me
yet. What did it mean? This
> day unlike other days, meaning
> like all days. Gold leafed
> letters pressed into cowhide

spelled my name. A present
for me, ten years old. Sent from
the printer and everything. I
carefully cut the box. Breathed. I
needed to understand. It said
something besides *Holy Bible*

> and my name. Something everyone
> I knew said I needed. I pressed
> the cover and my name against

my nose. Something there. In
the killed cow skin with gold
leaf, to understand.

     I'm baffled still.
     Was it the day
     or the words?

VI.

No. There are no
     correspondances.

     Only apps and rhymes.
          Only symbols for the forest;

meaning for the withering
     grass and fading flowers.

     It's called "time." But
          that isn't there either.

VII.

In there was Isaiah yelling:
     "Every valley shall be exalted,
     and every mountain and hill
     shall be made low: and
     the crooked shall be
     made straight, and
     the rough places plain."

Yes, and then . . .
        Time stops.
                Symbols fade.

                Words wither.
And nothing
        shall connect

                with nothing.

WHAT REMAINS WHEN DISBELIEF HAS GONE?

The thoroughly secular poet Philip Larkin wrote,

> But superstition, like belief, must die,
> And what remains when disbelief has gone?

In the poem, entitled "Church Going," Larkin has gone into a small church just to take a look around. He imagines a time beyond his own, when churches have entirely lost their current meaning to people. In that future, he asks,

> . . . will dubious women come
> To make their children touch a particular stone;
> Pick simples for a cancer; or on some
> Advised night see walking a dead one?

In other words, will the superstitions that Larkin considers created the need for churches in the first place remain after the present methods for assuaging the human impulse toward superstition wanes? Larkin muses,

> But superstition, like belief, must die,
> And what remains when disbelief has gone?

Larkin wrote his poem well before September 11th, 2001, when it became clear that neither belief nor superstition was anywhere near leaving the stage of human history.

Both Sides Now

Either a god gets retreaded
after some-millions miles
or there's gonna be a blowout.
It never fails.

    Fundamentalists get their jollies
    when the passel blows.
    Liberals just keep updating.
    holding to the road.

A retread is cheaper, after all,
than all the bother and fuss
of actually considering
ultimate sorts of stuff.

    Retread 'em
    or just keep runnin'.
    Finally, it's your choice.

Or, join me in enjoying
where freethinkers fit in.

THE CLOCK DOESN'T

Tick tick goes the clock,
but the mind doesn't do
        years. Only thoughts in
        the viscous rush of gone.

           Free floating, circling.
This after that. That then.

No. It's not a stream. No
        rocky bottom. No eddies.
           The mind doesn't do
years. Only shining spots.

There. There. Then.
        This before. This. This.

Right Down the Road

Right down the road
there's always something.

       Parthenon. Acropolis.
           Coliseum. Mall.

Right down the road
could be anything,

       only depending upon
           the place. Here is always

somewhere. And there.
There is somewhere

       someone can name.
           Only ask around.

THE WORK

Outgrow your god
        Outgrow yourself

Your call as
        Human is to

Outgrow your god
        Outgrow yourself

Outgrow your god
        Outgrow

INVITATION[15]

I come from consciousness
    and the sacred land of consciousness.
    Good folk, I you pray,

    for the sake of charity,
    come join with me
in the sacred land of consciousness

---

15. Icham of Irlaunde
    Ant of the holy londe
    Of Irlande.

    Gode sire, pray ich the,
    For of saynte charite,
    Come ant daunce wyt me
    In Irlaunde.

        —Anonymous, 14th century

OVER

Leaves on
        the limb
                blown down
in the wind,

green and
        quivering
                still one more
morning.

Incarnation News

We have
discovered that
     god is

indeed flesh

and dwells
among us
     indeed—in our

skulls and
bodies and
     whatever altogether

orbs, spheres,
     soft places
     rejoicing

in your experience

Dogma, a Song

Dogma, oh dogma,
shinin' so bright,
moldin' our views,
day 'n' night;

oh, dogma, stay strong
so that we might
avoid thinkin'—
day 'n' night.

With dogma beside us, we do find
purpose and truth, forever intertwined,
a creed we hold, a dogma burnin' true,
direction in life, it carries us through!

Dogma, oh dogma,
shinin' so bright,
moldin' our views,
day 'n' night;

oh, dogma, stay strong
so that we might
avoid thinkin'—
day 'n' night.

PICKING FLOWERS

When it comes down
to the weave—
          & always it does
                    come down
          to the weave—

when it gets
down to the weave—
          & always it does
          get there—

here, there

          in the threads
                    was, is
                    the answer
all along.

HAVING ARRIVED

When it arrives—
the caterpillar
        on the leaf—
                it's horizon,

                the infinite green,
        has no end . . .
the infinity of leaves.

When it arrives—
the caterpillar
        on the leaf—
                it's horizon,
perhaps it knows
        the leaves love
        their understanding;
love
        their grasp

of the world.

NOTHING NEITHER WAY

In a shadows' realm,
    where dreams unfold,
    no sovereign rules,
no throne in sight.

No specter doubts, whispers fade,
swallowed by night and certainty.

A tapestry, thread-less, bereft,
    no grand narratives,
    no Kosmic schemes,
atoms dancing without aspiration.

The poet's pen—cursor—hesitant,
    as unsure as astronomers lost in
    number's sway, tiny truths,
knocking on nihilism's door,

meaning's pipe dream
in a world of smoke.

Still, that subtle call persists,
    breathless, a transient face
    longing to blaze, possibilities
insisting on a flickering trace.

Though the void stares back,
    empty gazes are burning prize,
    yearning amidst life's intricate embrace.
Ride the storm, gather fragments.

Purposes, fragmented
       but real,
      in art, in love,
the connections we dare.

TULIP PETALS

No, I'm not worried that
     the tulip's petals fell.
          The violent purple

of it's coming to be
     reminded us all of life
          returning. Now, not.

Possible History Lesson

Thinking beyond thought;
  saying beyond words—
a poet's dream of legends,

lore, fervor chronicled,
  adorned in a veil that
hints it might be truth,

    only a bit askew.
    Observe the crafted, rhythmic
    sway of verses, myths entwine,
      their stories playing tag

or tug-a-war.

    Every history is myth;
    every myth historical;
    every history mystical
    to those who believe.

Art in eternal dance, lives unwinding.
Sagas weave, but never
of themselves. Always
the fibers dyed before.
claiming fates' decree,
Unfolding realms, forever free.

Every history
can be rewritten.
More mystical,
less. We can

even make
mysticism
mythic and
myth
mystic.

        History is myth
        and mystical
        to its believers.

A Considered and Honest Opinion Concerning Death

That's it.

      I guess.

            Maybe not.

Who

      knows?

About the Author

Rev. Dr. David Breeden is a Unitarian Universalist minister and author. He has served as the Senior Minister at the First Unitarian Society of Minneapolis (FUS) since 2013. The First Unitarian Society of Minneapolis is a historic congregation with a long-standing tradition of congregational humanism, progressive thought, and social activism.

Dr. Breeden has an MFA from The Writers' Workshop at the University of Iowa, a Ph.D. from the Center for Writers at the University of Southern Mississippi, with additional study at Breadloaf and in writing and Buddhism at Naropa Institute in Boulder, Colorado. He also has a Master of Divinity from Meadville Lombard Theological School in Chicago.

As a scholar and author, Dr. Breeden has contributed to various publications, including essays, articles, and books. His works often challenge conventional beliefs and encourage critical thinking.

His published books include *A Little Book of Living Through the Day: Poems During a Pandemic*, *The Art of Prophecy*, *After the Bloody Mary Game: Living Into Humanism*, *Daodejing: a translation*, *Deep Fragrance (in the Valley of the Void)*, *News from the Kingdom of God: Meditations on the Gospel of Thomas*, *They've Played for Timelessness (with Chips of When)*, *This is Just to Say, Meditations on a Theme by William Carlos Williams*.

Dr. Breeden is an adjunct faculty member of United Theological School in the Twin Cities and Chairs the Education Committee of the American Humanist

Association. He is a professional member of PEN and is an Associate member of the Institute for American Religious and Philosophical Thought (IARPT). He was the 2023 recipient of the Distinguished Service Award by the American Humanist Association.

Many Things—are fruitless—
'Tis a Baffling Earth—

—Emily Dickinson, #614

.

SHANTI ARTS

NATURE ▪ ART ▪ SPIRIT

Please visit us online
to browse our entire book catalog,
including poetry collections and fiction,
books on travel, nature, healing, art,
photography, and more.

Also take a look at our highly regarded art
and literary journal, *Still Point Arts Quarterly*,
which may be downloaded for free.

www.shantiarts.com

www.ingramcontent.com/pod-product-compliance
Lightning Source LLC
Chambersburg PA
CBHW072145090426
42739CB00013B/3286